Scholastic Children's Books
Euston House, 24 Eversholt Street,
London NW1 1DB, UK

A division of Scholastic Ltd
London ~ New York ~ Toronto ~ Sydney ~ Auckland
Mexico City ~ New Delhi ~ Hong Kong

Written by Stephanie Clarkson
Line illustrations by Diana Hill
Produced for Scholastic by 38a The Shop

Published in the UK by Scholastic Ltd, 2016
© Scholastic Children's Books, 2016

ISBN 978 1407 17088 6

Printed in China

2 4 6 8 10 9 7 5 3

www.scholastic.co.uk

Picture credits:

Front cover: (top left, top right and bottom middle) David M. Benett/Getty*; (bottom left) Dave J Hogan/Getty*; (bottom right) Craig Barritt/Getty*;
p6: (left to right) David M. Benett/Getty*; Ki Price/Corbis; Shirlaine Forrest/Getty*; David M. Benett/Getty*; Karwai Tang/Getty*; Efren S. Landaos/Press Line Photos/Corbis; Chris Jackson/Getty*; Ian West/Pa Wire/ZUMA Press/Corbis; Gabriel Olsen/Getty*; Jesse Grant/ Getty*; P10: 145/Saul Gravy/Ocean/Corbis; p12: David M. Benett/Getty*; p13: (t) Splash News; (b) David M. Benett/Getty*; p14: (t and m) David M. Benett/Getty*; (b) Anthony Harvey/Getty*; p16: Jesse Grant/Getty*; p18: (both) Jesse Grant/Getty*; p20: Laura Cavanaugh/Getty*; p21: (t) Jesse Grant/Getty*; (b) Tibrina Hobson/Getty*; p22: (t) Mireya Acierto/Getty*; (m) Mike Windle/Getty*; (b) Jason LaVeris/Getty*; p24: Thos Robinson/Getty*; p25: (t) Andrew Toth/Getty*; p26: (t) Craig Barritt/Getty*; (m) Jon Furniss/Corbis; (b) David M. Benett/Getty*; p28: David M. Benett/Getty*; p29: (t) Samir Hussein/Getty*; (b) Stuart C. Wilson/Getty*; p30: (t) Neil P. Mockford/Getty*; (m) Brian Rasic/Getty*; (b) See Li/Demotix/Corbis; p32: Craig Barritt/Getty*; p33: (t) James Higgins; (b) Shirlaine Forrest/Getty*; p34: (t) David M. Benett/Getty*; (m) INF Photo; (b); Shirlaine Forrest/Getty*; p36: Brent N. Clarke/Getty*; p37: (t) Dave Kotinsky/Getty*; (b) Daniel Zuchnik/Getty*; p38 (t) Jesse Grant/Getty*; (m) Kimberly White/Getty*; (b) Ben Gabbe/Getty*; p40: Craig Barritt/Getty*; p41: (t) David M. Benett/Getty*; (b) Craig Barritt/Getty*; p42: (t) Thos Robinson/Getty*; (b) David M. Benett/Getty*; p43: BSIP/Getty*; p44 David M. Benett/Getty*; p45: (t) Atlantic Images; (m) David M. Benett/Getty*; p46: (t) David M. Benett/Getty*; (m) PicSol/Retna Ltd./Corbis; (b) Karwai Tang; p48: @gotpaptv; p49: (t) Jason Merritt/Getty*; (b) Paul Archuleta/Getty*; p50: (t) Keipher McKennie/Getty*; (m) Unique Nicole /Getty*; (b) Jesse Grant/Getty*; p52: (t) David M. Benett/Getty*; p53: (t) Mike Coppola/Getty*; (b) Chelsea Lauren/Getty*; p54: (t) Brian Rasic/Getty* p55: (t) Michael Tullberg/Getty*; (b) Jerod Harris/Getty*; p56: (t) Karwai Tang/Getty*; (m) David M. Benett/Getty*; p57: (t) Mike Pont/Getty*; (b) FilmMagic/Getty*; p58 (b) David M. Benett/Getty*; p59 (t) David M. Benett/Getty*; p60 (t) Anthony Stanley/Retna Ltd/Retna Ltd./Corbis; (ml) David M. Benett/Getty*; p61: (mr) Ben A. Pruchnie/Getty*; (ml) See Li/Demotix/Corbis; (b) Nick Harvey/Getty*; p62: (t) Mark Sagliocco/Getty*; (b) Jörg Carstensen/dpa/Corbis; p63: (t) Gabriel Olsen/Getty*; (b) Michael Tullberg/Getty*; p64: (t) Angela Weiss/Getty*; (mr) Donato Sardella/Getty*; (ml) Amanda Edwards/Getty*;; (b) Mike Windle/Getty*; p65: (t) Angela Weiss/Getty*; (mr) Rob Kim/Getty*; (ml) C Brandon/Getty*;; (b) Michael Loccisano/Getty*; p66: (t) Jason Oxenham/Getty*; (ml) Araya Diaz/Getty*; (b) Chris Jackson/Getty*; p67: (t) Caroline McCredie/Getty*; (mr) Matthew Eisman/Getty*; (b) Kristy Sparow /Getty*; p72: (tl) Kevin Winter/Getty*; (tr) Mike Windle/Getty*; (b) Dave J Hogan/Getty*; p73: (tl) Mike Marsland/Getty*; (tr) Gabriel Olsen/Getty*; (b) Jason LaVeris/Getty*; p76: (tl) Rodrigo Vaz/ Getty*; (tr) David M. Benett/Getty*; (tl, tr, b) Creative RF/Getty*; p77: (l-r) Rachel Murray/Getty*; John Sciulli/Getty*; Kevin Mazur/Getty*; Chelsea Lauren/Getty*; David M. Benett/Getty*; Tim P. Whitby/Getty*; David M. Benett/Getty*; Peter Larsen/Getty*; p78: (t) Noam Galai/Getty*; (ml) Joseph Okpako/Getty*; (mr) Michael Tullberg/Getty*; (b) Paul Archuleta/Getty*; p79: (tl) Mike Windle /Getty*; (ml) Jonathan Leibson/Getty*; (mr) Steve Granitz/Getty*; (bl) FilmMagic/Getty*; (br) Barry King/Getty*; p80: (l-r) Amanda Edwards/Getty*; Cindy Ord/Getty*; Noam Galai/Getty*; Kirstin Sinclair/Getty*; FilmMagic/Getty*; Stuart C. Wilson/Getty*; Vincent Sandoval/Getty*; Shirlaine Forrest/Getty*; David Livingston/Getty*; Taylor Hill /Getty*; Thos Robinson/Getty*; Jesse Grant/Getty*; Matthew Eisman/Getty*; Mireya Acierto/Getty*; p81: (t) Joseph Okpako/Getty*; David M. Benett/Getty*; Noam Galai/Getty*; Jerod Harris/Getty*; Shirlaine Forrest/Getty*; David M. Benett/Getty*; Gareth Cattermole/Getty*; David M. Benett/Getty*; Imeh Akpanudose/Getty*; Dave J Hogan Kirstin Sinclair/Getty*; Kimberly White/Getty*; Michael Tullberg/Getty*; p82: (tl) Tibrina Hobson/Getty*; (br) Neil Mockford/Alex Huckle/Getty*; p83: (br) Joseph Okpako/Getty*; p84: (b) FilmMagic/Getty*; p85: (tl) Frazer Harrison/AMA2015/Getty*; (bl): Jerod Harris/Getty*; (br) PicSol./Retna Ltd./Corbis; p86: (l-r) Mike Marsland/Getty*; Keipher McKennie/Getty*; Dave J Hogan/Getty*; David M. Benett/Getty*; David M. Benett/Getty*; David M. Benett/Getty*; Brian Rasic/Getty*; Michael Tullberg/Getty*; David M. Benett/Getty*; Karwai Tang/Getty*; Samir Hussein/Getty*; Karwai Tang/Getty*; Joseph Okpako/Getty*; David M. Benett/Getty*; David M. Benett/Getty*; Gabriel Olsen/Getty*; Chelsea Lauren/Getty*; David M. Benett/Getty*; Kevin Winter/Getty*; FilmMagic/Getty*; Gabriel Olsen/Getty*; David M. Benett/Getty*; David M. Benett/Getty*; Araya Diaz/Getty*; Mike Marsland/Getty*; Steve Granitz/Getty*; Samir Hussein/Getty*; p90: (l-r) Gabriel Olsen/Getty*; Ian Gavan/Getty*; David M. Benett/Getty*; p91: (l-r) Michael Tullberg /Getty*; Alex B. Huckle /Getty*; Craig Barritt /Getty*; p92: Donald Bowers/Getty*; p93: (t) Allen J. Schaben /Getty*; (m) Photofusion /Getty*; (b) Anthony Harvey /Getty*;

p13: (m) Tanya Burr/YouTube; p17: (all) MagicAnimalClub/YouTube; p21: (m) Rosanna Pansino/YouTube; p25: (m) SprinkleofGlitter/YouTube; (b) SprinkleofChatter/YouTube; p29 (m) Zoella/YouTube; p33: (m) ThatcherJoe/YouTube; p37: (ml) On Air with Ryan Seacrest/YouTube; (mr) The White House/YouTube; p41: (m) RayawasHere/YouTube; p45: (b) PointlessBlogVlogs/YouTube; p49: (m) Jennxpenn/YouTube; p52: (b) Inthefrow/YouTube; p54 (b) AmazingPhil/YouTube; p56: (b) ItsWayPastMyBedTime/YouTube; p58: (t) KSI/YouTube; p59 (b) Bubzbeauty/YouTube; p60: (mr) Jazzybum/YouTube; (m) MoreTDM/YouTube; p61: (t) Tyrannosauruslexxx/YouTube; p66: (mr) バイリンガール英会話 Bilingual Chika/YouTube; p67: (ml) BooksandQuills/YouTube; (mr) CutiePieMarzia/YouTube; p68 (tl and r): EveryDayJim/YouTube; (b) Shaytards/YouTube; p69: (tl) PointlessBlogVlogs/YouTube; (tr) Jennxpenn/YouTube; (b) Patricia Bright/YouTube; p70: (t) FunForLouis/YouTube; (m) Tyler Oakley/Youtube; (b) Miranda Sings/YouTube; p71: (t) Bailey/YouTube (ml) MoreMarcus/YouTube (mr) Zoella/YouTube (b) PointlessBlog/YouTube; p74: (l) The Lean Machines/YouTube (r) The Lean Machines/YouTube; p75: (t) Deanne Love/YouTube (bl) The Body Coach/YouTube; (br) SaskiasDansSchool/YouTube; p76: (b) The Michalaks/YouTube; p77: (t) Itsjudytime/YouTube; p79: (tr) Ben Phillips/YouTube; p82: (t) Thatcher Joe/YouTube; (bl) Joey Graceffa/YouTube; p83: (t) Melissa55/YouTube; (bl) Zoella/YouTube; p84: (t) ThatcherJoe/YouTube; p87: (l-r) The Slow Mo Guys/YouTube; Tom Fletcher/YouTube; PointlessBlog/YouTube; FunforLouis/YouTube; Lisa Eldridge/YouTube; Stampylonghead/Youtube; p88: (t) Thatcher Joe/YouTube; (m) Rosanna Pansino/YouTube; (b) Thatcher Joe/YouTube; p89: (tl) Grace Helbig/YouTube; (tr) Brooklyn and Bailey/YouTube; (b) Jennxpenn/YouTube

Vlog On...

MORE FROM YOUR TOP VLOGGERS

■SCHOLASTIC

Contents

Nice To Vlog You!

Welcome to the wonderful world of vloggers, vlogging and vlogs.

You have this book for one of the following reasons:

 1. You are a major fan of vlogging.

2. You have never heard of vlogging and are curious to know what all the fuss is about.

3. You asked your parents if you could start your own YouTube channel and they handed you this instead.

No matter how *Vlog On!* has ended up in your hands, you've struck gold. Packed with facts, stats, tips and trivia, you now have the good fortune to possess a treasure trove of knowledge for would-be content creators, fans of superstar vloggers or those who just want to get to grips with the sizzling new media that's firing up the Internet.

Turn the page to...

- Discover the vlogging communities in the UK, the US and around the world.

- Tap into the creativity of the best vlogging personalities.

- Find out where to catch up with these YouTube superstars.

- Read about the hottest memes and trends.

- Enjoy great photos of your fave online stars.

- Test your knowledge with quick quizzes and questionnaires.

- Learn about viral vids and vines.

- Work up your own vlogging ideas for now or the future.

A Word To The Wise

Vlogging is great fun, but the Internet can pose dangers. The first thing that you need to know before you get online is how to use technology responsibly.

Before you start posting or think about setting up your own channel, get permission from your parent or guardian first. Agree the basic ground rules and show them the content that you're planning to share.

Warning signs!

If someone online asks you to keep your chats secret, wants you to send them pictures of yourself or use a webcam in a way that makes you feel uncomfortable, or even suggests that you could be in trouble if you tell someone about them, talk to a your parent or carer immediately.

Think!

Once something is made public online it can come back to haunt you. If you wouldn't be happy with a parent, teacher or guardian seeing a comment you've written or a clip you've filmed, don't post it.

Sad but true!

Not everyone online is who they say they are.

Want to speak confidentially about something that is worrying you? Call Childline free on 0800 1111, or visit childline.org.uk.

Top tips for staying safe

1. Never post any personal information online. This includes your real name, address, the name of your school, your email address and phone numbers.

2. Beware of posting footage that could clearly identify you – such as revealing images of your home or shots of yourself wearing school uniform.

3. Ask a trusted adult to set your privacy settings to the max. Make sure that they review them regularly.

4. Set strong passwords to make sure that your account is as secure as possible. Share them with your parents or guardians, but never give them out to anyone else.

5. Don't befriend people you don't know and never meet up with anyone that you've met online. Speak to an adult straightaway if anyone suggests that you do.

6. Be respectful of other people's opinions online. Don't post mean comments about them or their content and don't get into arguments with other Internet users.

7. When you are watching other people's vlogs, take care to avoid clips that are not appropriate for you. Vlogging is spontaneous and fast moving, so even a channel that you know well might occasionally post footage that is unsuitable for your age group. If in doubt, click away.

8. When you go on a new site, check out the rules and minimum age requirement. Never upload clips or pictures if you are younger than the age. If you're too young to start vlogging now – don't worry! Creating a great vlog takes a long time. This book is packed with tips to help you plan your future debut.

#MAINSTREAM

HA HA!

THE WORD 'VLOG' IS A COMBINATION OF THE WORDS 'VIDEO' AND 'BLOG'. IT'S A SHORT CLIP CONTAINING THE THOUGHTS AND OPINIONS OF THE CREATOR – OR VLOGGER – FILMED BY THEMSELVES AND POSTED ONLINE.

Q&A

You probably knew this already, right? These days if we're not vlogging ourselves, we're watching vlogs, talking about them or even buying merchandise related to our favourite vlogging stars.

During the last couple of years, vlogging has gone mainstream. What started out as a few people talking at a screen in their bedrooms has become the hottest media trend ever! It's a brilliant way to share our ideas, thoughts and talents with the world. There are countless reasons that vlogs have caught on – we can use them to amuse, entertain or to educate ourselves. Watching up-to-the-minute firsthand footage make us feel connected, both to the creator and to other like-minded viewers.

The brilliant thing about vlogging is that anyone can do it. Unlike radio, TV or magazines, you don't need specific training or to try and get selected for a job. All you need is an idea, a camera, a computer and an Internet connection.

The most successful vlogging stars now have billions of people watching them. They have money, popularity, fame and get to do a thing they love. The biggest names have bagged sellout book and theatre tours, clothing lines, merchandising deals and even movie roles. Some even have the ear of the world's most powerful people.

INTRODUCING
ME!

Vlogging has truly revolutionized the way we communicate and connect. For the determined and talented few, filming and posting online can open many doors and even lead to a full-time career. When Zoella posted her first video, '60 Things In My Bedroom', she had no idea where it was going to lead her. Where will your passion for vlogging take you?

I love vlogging because…

My ultimate vlogging goal is…

In five years' time I would like to be…

Totally Tanya

CHECK MY DEETS!

Vlogger ID:	Tanya Burr
Real name:	Tanya Burr
Born:	June 1989, Norfolk, UK
Star sign:	Gemini
Achievements:	The Global Goals Ambassador for the United Nations; on the judging panel for *Elle* Beauty Awards; cover girl for *Glamour* magazine.
Significant others:	Husband, Jim Chapman
Most likely to say:	"Hi guys!"
Often seen:	Taking walks on windswept Norfolk beaches.

I'm known for...

- Make-up tutorials – posts showing how to create a hot look, step-by-step.

- 'Get Ready With Me' – posts showing me prepping for an event or party.

*Awww cute!
My miniature Dachshund, Martha!*

Sooo excited about...

- My make-up line, Tanya Burr Cosmetics.

- A recent meeting with casting directors in LA – I want to secure a film role!

- Life as a newly-wed.

*Love him!
My husband, Jim.*

U.S.P. *That's Unique Selling Point, peeps!*

Tanya is successful because she's a real woman who makes the best of what she has. Her fans can count on her to be honest and down to earth.

Beauty By You

Tanya wasn't afraid to learn from others. She began vlogging in the evenings on the advice of her then boyfriend, now husband, Jim Chapman's make-up artist sisters. She also appeared in their clips in order to learn more from them.

Impressed by Tanya's attitude? Here's your chance to use her as inspiration...

Tanya inspires me because...

Her most watchable vlogs are...

My beauty vlog would be called...

My signature look is...

Did you know?

Tanya has always set herself goals – whether it be small targets to enhance her quality of life, such as reading more books, or longer term career goals. Tan's latest professional ambition is to secure a film role by the end of 2016 and she's been having acting lessons in order to make it happen. Goal setting is a great way to make sure that you always keep moving forward.

Top vlogging tip

"Good lighting, a cute top and a smile."

Create a brand logo

VISUALIZE YOUR OWN BEAUTY LINE!

How would your packaging look?

USE PENS TO STYLE UP THESE TEMPLATES!

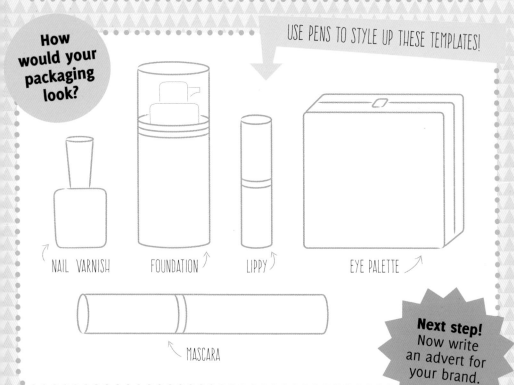

NAIL VARNISH

FOUNDATION

LIPPY

EYE PALETTE

MASCARA

Next step! Now write an advert for your brand.

Like Tanya's content? *Check out...*

- Pixiwoo
- Vivianna Does Makeup
- Fleur de Force
- Lisa Eldridge
- Beauty Crush
- Michelle Phan

Vlogger ID:	Stampy Longhead
Real name:	Joseph Garrett
Born:	December, 1990, Hampshire, UK
Star sign:	Sagittarius
Achievements:	Launching spinoff educational series 'Wonder Quest' with Maker Studios; featured panelist at MineCon.
Significant others:	Girlfriend Bethany Bates, aka Sqaishey Quack
Most likely to say:	"Yaaaay, I got a baby sheep!"
Often seen:	In his bedroom behind a microphone.

CHECK MY DEETS!

I'm known for...

- 'Let's Play' videos – everything from Minecraft and Terraria to Disney Infinity, Lego The Hobbit and Doki-Doki Universe.

- Squid and Stampy – gaming quests with my pal, David.

With Sqaishey at Disney World!

Sooo excited about...

- Going to more conventions and interacting with my fans.
- Seeing 'Wonder Quest' brought into schools.

U.S.P. That's Unique Selling Point, peeps!

My reclining gaming chair!

Stampy's upbeat delivery sets him apart from a sea of online gamers. His posts are family friendly and funny, packed with elements that kids enjoy.

Your Game!

Stampy loves playing 'sandbox' games like Minecraft because they engage the player, giving them the freedom to create their own worlds. He puts his success down to the fact that he's enjoying himself while he vlogs. There is something irresistible about watching somebody have so much fun!

Impressed by Stampy's enthusiasm? Here's your chance to use him as inspiration...

Stampy inspires me because...

His most watchable vlogs are...

My favourite video game is...

I like it because...

Did you know?

Stampy fell into vlogging by accident. He studied video production at university and spent a lot of time on YouTube, doing gaming reviews. He began recording his 'Let's Play' series just for fun. When he noticed how much people loved them, he went all out to make his content big, bright and family friendly.

Top vlogging tip

"If someone is rude or unkind to you when you're gaming, block them straightaway!"

Think of your favourite video game. Can you design a brand new character, vehicle or element to go in it?

Draw it in here.

Next step!
The next time that you play, have a go at narrating your progress on-screen.

DON`T FORGET TO NAME YOUR CREATION!

Like Stampy's content? *Check out...*

- iBallisticSquid
- Sqaishey Quack
- The Diamond Minecart
- Magic Animal Club
- Amy Lee33
- Yogscast

Really Rosanna!

Vlogger ID:	Nerdy Nummies
Real name:	Rosanna Pansino
Born:	June 1985, Seattle, USA
Star sign:	Gemini
Achievements:	Cookbook featured on the *New York Times* bestseller list; winner of the Shorty Award for Best Food in Social Media, has made Kermit cookies with Miss Piggy.
Significant others:	Younger sister Molly (or Mo)
Most likely to say:	"Hey guys, it's Ro!"
Often seen:	Browsing Target and other shops searching for ingredients.

CHECK MY DEETS!

I'm known for...

- 'How To...' videos – gaming, comic and movie themed cakes, desserts and treats.

- Food challenges – testing out ideas with my sister, Mo.

Ooooh! New kitchen! Check out my mega-fridge!

Soooo excited about...

- Seeing where my music career goes following my debut track *Perfect Together*.

- Touring with my cookbook.

OMG! My book signing in LA.

U.S.P. *That's Unique Selling Point, peeps!*

Rosanna's Nerdy Nummies vlogs are unique because they combine two different genres – gaming and baking.

21

What's Cookin'?

At the start of her vlogging journey Rosanna had to make some tough choices. She had moved to Hollywood to pursue a movie career, and was doing well. She decided to quit regular acting work, however. She wanted to focus full-time on making her YouTube channel successful instead.

Impressed by Rosanna's dedication? Here's your chance to use her as inspiration...

Rosanna inspires me because...

Her most watchable vlogs are...

My cooking vlog would be called...

I would greet viewers by...

Did you know?

When she was younger, Rosanna saved ten per cent of her paychecks from every part-time job. This meant that when the time came, she was able to buy good lighting and camera equipment. Rosanna is now one of the world's top earning vlogging stars. She has even been named in *Forbes* magazine's list of top ten YouTube earners. In 2015, she made over £1.7 million!

Top vlogging tip

"Make content you are passionate about. Inspiration comes from everywhere."

Write a vlogging script to introduce your favourite recipe.

Think about...

Why is it your favourite?

What makes it so tasty?

Is it easy or hard to bake?

Next step!
Try talking through each step of the recipe next time you make it.

Like Nerdy Nummies' content? *Check out...*

- My Cupcake Addiction
- How to Cook That
- Cupcake Jemma
- Jamie Oliver
- Laura in the Kitchen
- Deliciously Ella

Look! It's Louise

Vlogger ID:	Sprinkle Of Glitter
Real name:	Louise Pentland
Born:	April 1985, Northampton, UK
Star sign:	Taurus
Achievements:	Sell-out 'Louise Live' tour; interviewed Ed Miliband during the last UK election; has designed a plus-size clothing range for SimplyBe.
Significant others:	BFF Zoe Sugg and daughter Darcy, aka Baby Glitter
Most likely to say:	"I feel very swishy!"
Often seen:	On the plane to Seattle – her happy place.

CHECK MY DEETS!

I'm known for...

- Big topics – I regularly discuss important issues that come up in viewer comments.

- 'ChummyChatter' – posts with my bestie Zoella.

In the pink for Cancer Research UK!

Sooo excited about...

- Putting more personality into my videos.
- Vlogging more on Sprinkle Of Chatter.
- Focussing on the things I can control – myself, Darcy and work.

U.S.P. *That's Unique Selling Point, peeps!*

Viewers love to listen to Louise because she talks good sense. She shares on every topic, whether it's loneliness or body confidence, with honesty and humour.

Annual 'Careoke' sesh with Zoe!

Incredible You!

Louise Pentland really does sprinkle glitter into the lives of her viewers. With her raucous laugh, fondness for all things pink and positive messages about the importance of friendship, family and love, she's guaranteed to add a touch of sparkle to your day.

Impressed by Louise's zest for life? Here's your chance to use her as inspiration...

Louise inspires me because...

Her most watchable vlogs are...

The best thing about her is...

My BFFs are great because...

Did you know?

Louise loves the sense of community that comes with vlogging. She has made some great friends along the way, including Zoella and Marie BitsAndClips. She rarely finds negative comments on her vlog entries and is impressed by the way her subscribers are kind and encouraging to each other, too.

Top vlogging tip

"Don't steal ideas. Look at what's trendy, then give it your own spin."

My mind map

Use this page to kickstart some good feelings about yourself and your life. Create a 'mind map' of positivity. Put yourself in the centre, then fill the branches with motivating thoughts and the names of people or things that make you happy.

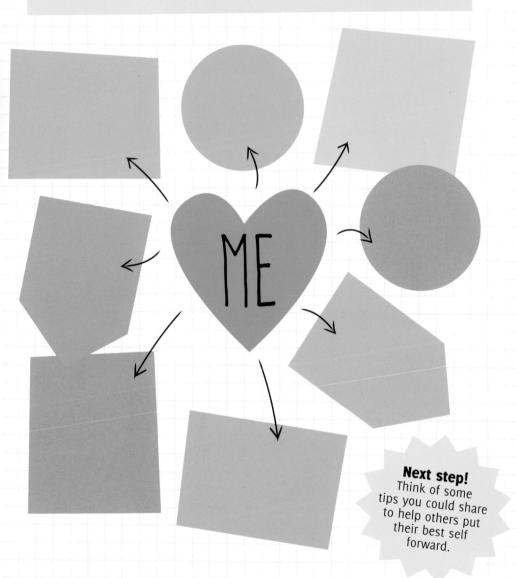

Next step! Think of some tips you could share to help others put their best self forward.

Like Sprinkle Of Glitter's content? *Check out...*

- What's Up Moms
- BitsAndClips
- Mums Eye View
- SacconeJolys
- Fleur de Force
- Caroline Hirons

So Zoella

CHECK MY DEETS!

Vlogger ID:	Zoella
Real name:	Zoe Sugg
Born:	March 1990, Lacock, UK
Star sign:	Aries
Achievements:	Fastest selling debut novelist since records began; 10 million YouTube subscribers and rising; voted favourite vlogger at 2015 Nickelodeon Kids' Choice Awards.
Significant others:	Brother Joe and boyfriend, Alfie Deyes
Most likely to say:	"Cuuuuute!"
Often seen:	Strolling in the Brighton Lanes.

I'm known for...

- Haul videos – posts where I go through my recent and fave buys.
- '#AskZoella' – interactive posts where I answer questions from my followers.

Percy loves eskimo-kisses!

Sooo excited about...

- Recent planning meetings with the Zoella beauty team.
- Being immortalized as a Madame Tussaud's waxwork.
- Doing more casual, informal and intimate meet-ups with my fans.

It's me! Or is it?

U.S.P. *That's Unique Selling Point, peeps!*

Zoella's sunny disposition coupled with her chatty presenting style and great content ensure that she is both watchable and lovable.

29

Presenting... You!

A talented presenter, Zoella can vlog about anything with style. Her relaxed, on-screen presence is all the more impressive given that she is naturally shy and suffers from crippling anxiety and panic attacks. Zoe worked extremely hard to perfect her craft, filming herself over and over until she got used to speaking on camera.

Impressed by Zoella's presentation skills? Here's your chance to use her as inspiration...

Zoella inspires me because...

Her most watchable vlogs are...

My vlogging user name would be...

I would greet viewers by...

Top vlogging tip

"Have fun. ... Don't worry about not feeling confident at first, confidence is something you learn and progress with."

Did you know?

Even award-winning vloggers have ups and downs. Zoella has therapy to help her with her anxiety. She says that sometimes, just like her *Girl Online* creation Penny, she feels like throwing her laptop in her wardrobe and shutting everything out.

Long before you start a vlog, it's important to work on your presenting style. You can film yourself and watch the footage without posting it online. You can also practise in front of a mirror.

1 — Plan Ahead

Seek inspiration – watch lots of different styles of vlogs so that you work out what works and why. List the vloggers that you think have a fab presenting style.

2 — Prepare

Outfit – choose clothes that make you feel good to boost your confidence. Describe your favourite outfit:

Nerves – relaxation exercises will calm you before filming. Note down your most helpful relaxation tip.

3 — Practise

Voice – use your natural voice – this isn't the time to try out a deep, voiceover tone or a cool accent. Warm up your voice by humming a tune with your mouth open or shut. Drink lots of water to help your tone and stop your throat from drying out.

Eye contact – look straight at the lens, not at the screen.

Next step!
Practise talking to camera while sitting, standing or walking.

Like Zoella's content? *Check out...*

- Bethany Mota
- Niomi Smart
- Lily Pebbles
- Gabriella Lindley
- Freddy My Love
- Dulce Candy

Just Joe!

CHECK MY DEETS!

Vlogger ID:	ThatcherJoe
Real name:	Joseph (Joe) Sugg
Born:	September 1991, Lacock, UK
Star sign:	Virgo
Achievements:	Broke Amazon's sell-out records with sales of his DVD *Joe And Caspar Hit The Road*; graphic novelist; voted Best British Vlogger at Radio 1 Teen Awards 2015.
Significant others:	Sister, Zoe, and BFF and housemate, Caspar Lee
Most likely to say:	"I am NOT a daily vlogger!"
Often seen:	Buying mosquito repellent.

I'm known for...

- Impressions – from the Muppets to Mr Bean and Jack Sparrow, they're all in my repertoire.

- Pranks – prank calls, roommate revenge pranks, jokes featuring tinfoil, showers and balloons.

Vicious Fish!

Sooo excited about...

- More vlogs from trips around the world with Caspar and Oli.

- Getting back into doodling.

'Jaspar' on the road!

U.S.P.

That's Unique Selling Point, peeps!

No one is happier making a fool of himself on camera than Joe, from slips, trips and falls to verbal gaffs – Joe is the class clown come good.

Tell Us a Story!

Joe Sugg has a great sense of storytelling and drama, as witnessed in his ability to narrate a vlog, tell a funny anecdote, do an impression or ramp up the suspense during a prank. This talent has seen the number of subscribers to his channel rocket! It has also allowed him to branch out with his first graphic novel.

Impressed by Joe's creativity?
Here's your chance to use him as inspiration...

ThatcherJoe inspires me because...

His most watchable vlogs are...

My channel would be called...

The prank I would most like to play is...

Did you know?

Joe knows that stories and content can be found anywhere in life. He will cleverly find points of interest for his viewers no matter whether he's showing firsthand what it's like to work as a roof thatcher, talking about a TV programme he's just watched or simply sharing the view from his window.

Top vlogging tip

"It's about the 3 Cs – consistency, collaboration and creativity."

Use these cells to sketch out a section of your own graphic novel.

- What's your novel called?
- Who is your main character?
- Where is your story set?

AND SO IT BEGAN...

TO BE CONTINUED...

Next step!
Plan where your story goes next. Add more detail to the world you have created.

Like ThatcherJoe's content? Check out...

- Caspar Lee
- Jim Chapman
- Oli White
- RomanAtwoodVlogs
- Ricky Dillon
- Marcus Butler

Tyler-Tastic!

CHECK MY DEETS!

Vlogger ID:	Tyler Oakley
Real name:	Tyler Oakley
Born:	March 1989, Michigan, USA
Star sign:	Aries
Achievements:	Star of documentary *Snervous*; continues to raise hundreds of thousands of pounds for charity; interviewed Michelle Obama and attended the White House to talk about health care.
Significant others:	Mum 'Queen Jackie', BFF and manager Korey Kuhl
Most likely to say:	"I literally cannot even!"
Often seen:	Having dance battles in his lounge.

I'm known for...

- Collabs – I love filming with other YouTubers.

- Fangirling – posts about my obsessions.

Talking health with Obama.

Sooo excited about...

- Continuing with my fab 'Psychobabble' podcast.

- Following the US presidential race.

Not remotely 'Snervous' as I introduce my documentary!

U.S.P. That's Unique Selling Point, peeps!

Tyler calls himself a 'professional over-sharer', willing to talk about the good and the bad. Fans love that he is not afraid to speak out on issues that matter to him.

Your Voice!

Tyler Oakley is determined to use his YouTube fame as a platform for good. He works tirelessly to give his fans the confidence to be themselves. He raises money for youth charities, champions the importance of education and the right to good healthcare, and talks about dealing with bullies.

Impressed by Tyler's passion? Here's your chance to use him as inspiration...

Tyler inspires me because...

His most watchable vlogs are...

The influential person I would most like to interview is...

I would ask them about...

Did you know?

Very few vloggers are as prolific as Tyler. Whether it's taking over the billboards of New York's Time Square or presenting at the Teen Choice Awards, the guy has become a mainstream celebrity! Tyler is an Internet trailblazer – constantly breaking down the barriers of what YouTubers can achieve.

Top vlogging tip

"Never give up! I was making videos for five years before I was able to make it my full-time job."

Which issue is closest to your heart? Pick one of the causes on this page, or think of your own. Now plan a vlog explaining why it matters to you. Make the most honest, fact-packed and persuasive case that you can.

Next step!
Think up some practical ways that you could help raise awareness for this cause.

Like Tyler's content? *Check out...*

- Troye Sivan
- Joey Graceffa
- CharlieIsSoCoolLike
- Marcus Butler
- Connor Franta
- Korey Kuhl

Lively Louis!

@streamcon
#streamcon

Vlogger ID:	FunForLouis
Real name:	Louis Cole
Born:	April 1983, Epsom, UK
Star sign:	Taurus
Achievements:	Visited 66 countries during January 2016; launched 'Find the Nomads' clothing range. Partnered with Discovery on a project to fly the globe.
Significant others:	Mum, Liz, Dad, Ben and sisters Hilary and Darcy
Most likely to say:	"Peace out."
Often seen:	Wandering through airports with a selfie stick.

CHECK MY DEETS!

I'm known for...

- 360° videos – incredible panoramic film clips.
- 'Learn With Louis' – posts where I try out everything from circus skills to tie-dye.

Cow-birthday-boy on a trip to New Mexico!

Sooo excited about...

- Adding to my ever-increasing total of countries visited.
- Making a relationship work while travelling with my girlfriend Raya.

U.S.P. *That's Unique Selling Point, peeps!*

Louis is one of the few true daily vloggers, but then he does have the whole world to provide his content. He also gets fellow travellers and viewers to introduce his clips!

Meeting fans at Vidcon

Your Trip!

Louis Cole has seen more of the world in the past year than some of us will see in a lifetime. From dancing in Cuba, to deep-sea diving in Langkawi and motorbiking through the Australian outback, Louis travels the globe, experiencing new cultures and people – filming everything along the way.

Impressed by Louis' globetrotting? Here's your chance to use him as inspiration...

Louis inspires me because...

His most watchable vlogs are...

The place I would most like to visit is...

My ideal travel companion would be...

Top vlogging tip

"Make sure your camera equipment is in your carry-on luggage when you fly."

Did you know?

Louis got a taste for travel from the holidays he spent with his parents. Now his success has inspired his folks to get online, too. His dad uploads fun cooking vlogs, while his mum likes to chat about daily life.

Plot your dream round-the-world trip on this map!

Which countries would you visit?

Use this page to write about a day trip or holiday that you've been on.
Where did you go? What was the scenery like?
Did you meet any local people? Describe your favourite experiences.

Next step!
The next time that you head out on a day trip, try filming your adventures.

Like Louis' content? *Check out...*

- Mr Ben Brown
- JacksGap
- Hey Nadine
- Dave Erasmus
- RayaWasHere
- The VagaBrothers

Absolutely Alfie

Vlogger ID:	PointlessBlog
Real name:	Alfie Deyes
Born:	September 1993, London, UK
Star sign:	Virgo
Achievements:	Almost 8 million subscribers to his channels; starred in the BBC3 Documentary *Rise Of The Superstar Vloggers*; bestselling author.
Significant others:	Sister, Poppy and girlfriend, Zoella
Most likely to say:	"Goooood morning, guys!!"
Often seen:	Walking Nala the pug on Hove seafront.

CHECK MY DEETS!

I'm known for...

- 'Challenge' videos – everything from eating hot chillies, trying not to laugh and blindfold drawing.

- Tag videos – fun clips that go around on YouTube where questions are posed to friends, loved ones and fellow vloggers.

'Zalfie' on the razz!

Sooo excited about...

- Being able to drive now that I've passed my test.
- Using the new camera equipment I bought on a recent trip to Dublin with Zoe.

U.S.P. That's Unique Selling Point, peeps!

Alfie loves vlogging and he does it with confidence. He doesn't worry about the haters – all he cares about is creating good content.

In my motor!

So Pointless!

Alfie's content is sometimes random, but always entertaining. He enjoys the freedom of doing as he pleases – if he fancies uploading a film showing himself dancing like a nutter in his kitchen, he can! Equally, he doesn't shy away from talking seriously about a subject from time to time. This is what makes his vlogs so interesting.

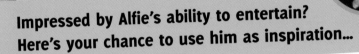

Impressed by Alfie's ability to entertain? Here's your chance to use him as inspiration...

Alfie inspires me because...

His most watchable vlogs are...

The video I wish Alfie would film is...

The most pointless thing I've ever done is...

Did you know?

Alfie began vlogging at the age of 16. He started with a clip of himself talking about fellow vlogger, Charlie McDonnell. The first time that Alfie earned more from his vlogging than he did at his Saturday job, he went and handed in his notice. Risky maybe, but luckily the gamble paid off.

Top vlogging tip

"Create a schedule so viewers know exactly when to tune in for a new video."

Use this page as a scrapbook. Fill it up with the random things that appeal to you. Which ones could you imagine yourself vlogging about?

STICK IN PHOTOS OR PICTURES

ADD FUNNY QUOTES

Next step!
Do a head-dump – write or draw anything that pops into your mind.

Like Alfie's content? *Check out...*

- NikiNSammy
- Jim Chapman
- DanIsNotOnFire
- CharlieIsSoCoolLike
- MyName'sChai
- AmazingPhil

Vlogger ID:	JennXPenn
Real name:	Jenn McAllister
Born:	July 1996, Pennsylvania, USA
Star sign:	Cancer
Achievements:	Starred in movie *Bad Night* and web series *First Times*; nominated for a Teen Choice Award for Choice Web Star.
Significant others:	Friends Andrea Russett, Arden Rose and Lauren Elizabeth
Most likely to say:	"I'm just not make-uply talented!"
Often seen:	Hanging with her pals at festivals like Coachella.

CHECK MY DEETS!

I'm known for...

- 'Top 10s' – top ten lists on any subject.
- Prank calling – daft phone calls to my friends and other YouTubers.

Cracking up!

Sooo excited about...

- Wearing more sweaters, playing more vinyl and taking more Polaroids.
- Wrapping filming for my new show.

U.S.P.

That's Unique Selling Point, peeps!

Jenn is the ultimate 'girl-next-door'. She's pretty, funny, interesting and loves both dressing up for special occasions and keeping it casual in jeans and jumpers.

With Lauren at the Bad Night film première

49

Original You!

Jenn started off by filming her normal life, then adding a crazy twist. She once made a snowman that turned evil and another time discovered a remote control that rewound her clip! Her life may have changed since she hit the Internet, but she continues to constantly come up with fresh posts. There's only one JennXPenn!

Impressed by Jenn's originality? Here's your chance to use her as inspiration...

Jenn inspires me because...

Her most watchable vlogs are...

If I could meet Jenn I'd ask...

I'm most comfortable when I'm...

Did you know?

Jenn knows only too well the risks of being online. In 2012, her three YouTube accounts were hacked. The hackers published her personal information online and stole credit card details. They were eventually caught, but Jenn has since described this as a "terrifying" period in her life.

Top vlogging tip

"Get inspired by attending YouTuber events."

Wait for a day when you're just hanging around doing normal stuff – maybe going to the supermarket, playing in the park or doing your homework. Now try to think up a fun sketch to film in that setting.

Next step!
Try editing your film and putting a funny soundtrack over the top of it.

Like Jenn's content? *Check out...*

- Andrea Russett
- Smosh
- AwesomenessTV
- Claudia Sulewski
- Charisma Kain
- MayBaby

If You Like... You'll Love

FASHION

If you like

In The Frow...

With her long, pastel-dyed locks and model appearance, British vlogger Victoria Magrath (aka In the Frow) stands out from the crowd. Victoria really knows her stuff – she even has a PhD in Fashion from the University of Manchester. After winning *Company* Magazine's Best Newcomer and Best Established Blog awards in 2012 and 2013, Victoria turned her attention to YouTube.

In just two years, In The Frow's style tips and fashion advice built up a following of nearly half a million subscribers. Victoria's clips feature tags and chats, collabs, shopping trips, unboxing and try-ons. She also loves travelling and has posted from Japan, Iceland, Ibiza and the Maldives.

Vlogger yoga sesh in Ibiza.

Fash pack peers:	Emily Sheldon; Hello October, Tamara Kalinic, Samantha Maria and Lexi A-N.
Most watched vids include:	'My Designer Shoe Collection', 'Prom' and 'Wedding GRWM'.
Onwards and upwards:	Nominated for *Glamour* Magazine's 2016 Woman of the Year Award.

Personal fashion philosophy

"I think that everyone should wear what they feel comfortable in and not pay attention to what others think about it. If more of us wore what we loved, we would have so many more experimental and unique people leading the way in fashion."

...you'll love **Evelina**

Bubbly Evelina Barry has over a million subscribers to her style channel! She films her clips in an LA apartment that she calls 'Unicorn HQ'. Evelina has long golden tresses and and loves showing off her favourite fashionable clothes picks. She insists that she's not about perfection, however. Instead Evelina thinks people like her because she can be 'honest and silly'.

With my gal, Jenn Im.

Evelina joined YouTube in May 2008 and has been steadily building her following ever since. She's so influential, she even gets to interview celebs about their style choices at the Oscars. Her first clips focussed on hair, but she quickly branched out into style. Nowadays she posts fashion lookbooks, hauls and 'Get Ready With Me' clips alongside style DIY and Q&As. Evelina is another true jetsetter! She has posted style vids from, London, Italy, New York and Amsterdam.

Fash pack peers:	Jenn Im, Bethany Mota, Chriselle Lim, Alexa Losey and StilaBabe.
Most watched vids include:	'10 Ways To Reinvent Your Look' and 'Get Ready With Me – Beach Style.'
Onwards and upwards:	Has just released a new line of jewellery called 'On the Road With Evelina'.

Personal fashion philosophy

"People are tired of the dictatorship. Fashion should be fun, accessible and for everybody."

If You Like...
You'll Love

If you like

Dan and Phil...

Dan Howell and Phil Lester are the UK's top Internet double act. Dan spent three years watching YouTube channels like CharlieIsSoCoolLike and Phil's AmazingPhil before setting up his own, DanIsNotOnFire. Both boys went to university – Phil graduated, but Dan dropped out when he was offered a full-time job. Both became passionate about their channels and eventually met through their vlogging community.

Dan and Phil started to pop up in each other's vids, increasing their traffic along the way. In 2013, they became the first Internet stars to be given their own slot on Radio 1. *The Internet Takeover* is a Sunday night show that they still host regularly. The lads are roomies too, living together in London.

Whiskery dudes.

Catch them on:	DanAndPhilGames, DanIsNotOnFire, AmazingPhil.
Most popular vids include:	'Dan And Phil Play Just Dance', 'Dan And Phil Punk Edit' and the 'PhilIsNotOnFire' series.
Great pipes, guys:	Dan and Phil love to belt out classic tracks by Britney, Muse and more.

HA! HA

YouTube musings

"I take stuff from my everyday life. Like, once I was bitten by a squirrel and I thought, 'well, there's a video!'" Phil

...you'll love **Rhett and Link**

Rhett McLaughlin and Charles Lincoln (Link) Neal met in junior school in North Carolina, USA. They have been best friends ever since, even sharing a room at college where they both studied engineering. Stardom however, beckoned from an early age. When they were 14, the boys wrote a screenplay for a film called *Gutless Wonders*. Sadly they never finished filming it, but they did use the material to make some clips many years later.

a! Ha!

FUNNIES!

Live on stage.

The guys are part of a new breed of 'Internetainers'. Besides their main channel, Rhett and Link came up with the idea for 'Good Mythical Morning'. Every morning they upload a new post, based on a daily TV talk show format. They also love teaming up with big companies to create viral marketing videos.

Catch them on:	Rhett and Link, Good Mythical Morning, Good Mythical More.
Most popular vids include:	'Will It Deep Fry?', 'Taste Test' and '6 Strangest Things Swallowed By A Shark'.
Great pipes, guys:	The lads' songbook includes 'Epic Rap Battle: Nerd Vs Geek', 'Get Off The Phone Song' and 'Rub Some Bacon On It'.

YouTube musings

"We're trying to widen people's expectations of what YouTube channels can hold." Link

If You Like...
You'll Love

If you like
Tom Fletcher and
Carrie Hope Fletcher...

When you're a famous musician or a West End star, you don't get a lot of time to write letters. So why not share your thoughts and feelings via video instead? McBusted front man Tom Fletcher vlogs under his own name while his talented sister Carrie has a channel called It'sWayPastMyBedTime.

The Fletcher siblings have made a whole series of vlogs. Each one was made expressly for the purpose of keeping each other updated on their hectic daily lives. Luckily the pair don't seem to mind the fact that the whole of YouTube get to hear and see what they're getting up to.

Sibling singsong!

Special sibling moments:	'The One When You Ruin *Les Mis*' (Tom's congratulations after Carrie's last show in *Les Mis*.)
Top vids:	'The One When I'm Awesomerer' and 'The One When We're Pregnant Again'.
And another thing:	The pair call their correspondence 'Dear Carrie/Tom: The One When...'

Best banter! → Tom: *Carrie's the manlier of us two.*

Carrie: *I really am! Actually I don't think I'm manlier. I think you're girlier.*

Brothers John and Hank Green are just as busy as the Fletchers. John is the bestselling author of *The Fault In Our Stars* and *Paper Towns*, while Hank is a scientist and entrepreneur. They set up their channel, VlogBrothers, in 2007. The posts began with them trying out a new project called Brotherhood 2.0. The idea was that they would stop all texting and phoning for one whole year, and communicate only by vlogging.

On stage at Vid Con.

John and Hank upload videos regularly, but they rarely share the screen. Each brother begins their clip by greeting the other directly, then continues to give their response to the opinions or thoughts the other one has raised. The Green boys talk about current affairs and their lives, in between trying to make each other laugh – just like most brothers. John and Hank are also responsible for setting up VidCon, the world's biggest online video conference.

Special sibling moments:	'The Reunion Vids' – clips where the boys actually get together.
Top vids:	'Top 10 Animal Power Moves' and '31 Jokes For Nerds'.
And another thing:	The hilarious strapline on their vlog reads: 'Vlog Brothers: Raising nerdy to the power of awesome!'

Best banter! → *Hank: John, what is your opinion on lamps?*

John: I am opposed to them.

BEST OF BRITISH

UK vloggers are producing some amazing content. Get to know the best of British, right here!

Vlogger ID:	KSI
Real name:	Olajide 'JJ' Olatunji
Born:	June 1993
Vlog Type	Gaming
Achievements:	Most powerful and wealthy British YouTuber according to *Forbes Magazine*; chart-topping rapper.

In the beginning KSI was just a boy who was 'big on gaming'. His first video had zero views, but he asked friends and family and put links on forums and people began taking notice. After a year he had 7,000 subscribers and after two this had shot up to 20,000. He decided to devote all his time to YouTube after asking a teacher if he should leave school – where he wasn't doing well – and discovering that he was already earning more than the teacher's salary. Since then, KSI has used his Internet stardom to kickstart his music career.

Quick triv

KSI's debut single as a solo artist was called:

a) Ferrari   b) Lamborghini   c) Bugatti

Vlogger ID:	Niomi Smart
Real name:	Niomi Smart
Born:	May 1992
Vlog Type	Lifestyle
Achievements:	Over 1.5 million subscribers to her YouTube channel.

Viewers love Niomi Smart! Her bubbly delivery and varied content – she covers health and fitness to homeware, fashion and beauty – means that she appeals to a wide audience. Niomi graduated from the University of Bristol with a law degree before starting her blog and then her own YouTube channel. The vlogger used to be the girlfriend of YouTuber Marcus Butler. Niomi continues to love life, often posting uplifting content to help her viewers stay healthy in body and mind.

Quick triv

When dating, Marcus and Naomi were known among the vlogging community as:

a) Narcus   b) Maomi   c) Smutler

Vlogger ID:	Jim Chapman
Real name:	Jim Chapman
Born:	December 1987
Vlog Type	Fashion and culture
Achievements:	Made *GQ Magazine*'s Best Dressed Man in Britain list in 2015; hosted the *Star Wars* première for YouTube.

Nobody is better connected than Jim Chapman. As well as being Tanya Burr's husband, he's brother to the Pixiwoo girls and the twin of John from The Lean Machines. On top of all this, Jim can also count Zoella and Alfie as two of his best mates! His '#Ask Jim' series and posts about daily life have been viewed hundreds of millions of times, allowing him to branch out into other media. Jim regularly appears on the Radio 1 show, *The Internet Takeover*, and recently presented a BBC3 documentary called *The Rise Of The Superstar Vloggers*.

Quick triv

Jim has a university degree in:

a) Geography   b) Sociology   c) Psychology

Vlogger ID:	BubzBeauty
Real name:	Lindy Tsang
Born:	December 1986
Vlog Type	Beauty
Achievements:	Entrepreneur Lindy has her own lines of clothing and make-up brushes.

Bubbly Lindy was bullied at school because of her looks and is now on a one-girl mission to help people grow in confidence. Lindy can turn her hand to any aspect of beauty – from creating smoky eye make-up to perfecting a basket braid up-do. Every month she outlines her faves, as well as posting her 'Girl Talk' and 'Inspirational' series. If you want to feel uplifted and positive, Lindy's channel is the place to go! In particular check out 'The Happiest Days Of Bubz' clips, where you'll find everything from her wedding proposal to news of her pregnancy.

Quick triv

Before getting married, Timothy Ng and Lindy had been dating for:

a) 10 weeks   b) 10 months   c) 10 years

Check your answers on page 96.

BEST OF BRITISH

We're shining the light on some more of the best British vloggers. Click through and see what the buzz is all about!

ANIMATION

Vlogger ID:	TomSka
Real name:	Thomas Ridgewell
Creates:	Funny animated videos on his channel including asdfmovie and Crash Zoom. Also produces webtoon 'Eddsworld'.
He once:	Got a piece of his dental brace caught in his throat.

DIY AND LIFE

Vlogger ID:	JazzyBum
Real name:	Jasmin
Creates:	Advice on everything from room décor, to study tips and perfecting the messy bun.
She once:	Filmed her day-to-day 'school routine' at Leeds university, while she was there studying physics.

GEEK CHIC

Vlogger ID:	CharlieIsSoCoolLike
Real name:	Charlie McDonnell
Creates:	Adorable geeky content on subjects like science and Doctor Who. Charlie tries to make his films fun and easy to follow.
He once:	Explained to his followers how sound works using the medium of song and a ukulele.

GAMING

Vlogger ID:	The Diamond Minecart/Dan TDM
Real name:	Daniel Middleton
Creates:	Mod showcases, mini adventures for Minecraft and 'Let's Play' series for games such as The Sims and Spore.
He once:	Had a YouTube channel solely dedicated to Pokémon.

BOOKS

Vlogger ID:	TyrannosaurusLexxx
Real name:	Lex Croucher
Creates:	A range of content, but is particularly passionate about reading. Her book reviews are funny and informative.
She once:	Posted a terrible vid called, 'I'm An Idiot'. She felt viewers should see it as a guide on how not to film a vlog post!

TRAVEL

Vlogger ID:	JacksGap
Real name:	Jack Harries
Creates:	Travel vlogs with a conscience. Jack and his twin brother Finn post fantastic videos from around the world, but always with an eye on the bigger picture.
He once:	Travelled around the world to surprise girlfriend Ella on her 19th birthday. Awww!

COMEDY

Vlogger ID:	Marcus Butler
Real name:	Marcus Butler
Creates:	Sketch based comedy. Marcus has filmed himself talking in voices we all use and showing YouTubers' selfie faces.
He once:	Set a world record with Alfie Deyes for the most bangles put on in thirty seconds by a team of two.

BEAUTY

Vlogger ID:	Pixiwoo
Real name:	Samantha Chapman and Nicola Chapman
Creates:	Make-up tutorials showing how to get A-lister looks and replicate film characters for parties and events.
They once:	Worked in the beauty industry. Sam was part of the Mac PRO team, while Nic worked on make-up counters in London.

U.S. OF VLOG

America is vlogging crazy! Each of these content creators is right at the top of their game.

Vlogger ID:	Michelle Phan
Real name:	Michelle Phan
Born:	April 1987
Vlog Type	Beauty and lifestyle
Achievements:	Won first Streamy ICON award; co-founded Ipsy, the world's largest online beauty community.

Michelle Phan is one inspiring girl. She had a difficult upbringing, but has gone on to create her own empire. Michelle's first clip was a seven minute tutorial on 'natural looking make-up'. The clip went viral, receiving 40,000 views in the first week! Michelle's posts have now received over a billion views, making her one of the most successful YouTubers in the world. She is a thoughtful, spiritual person who tries to inspire others. Michelle says her biggest dream was to help her mother retire early because she worked so hard to support her and her siblings.

Quick triv

Michelle was born in:

a) Orlando   b) San Francisco   c) Boston

Vlogger ID:	Lindsey Stirling
Real name:	Lindsey Stirling
Born:	September 1986
Vlog Type	Music
Achievements:	Named Artist of the Year at the 2015 YouTube Music Awards.

Violinist and performance artist Lindsey first appeared on screen in *America's Got Talent* in 2010. It wasn't until she began posting clips on YouTube however, that her career really took off. Viewers liked the way she combined her amazing musical talents with some impressive dance skills. Lindsey now has over 7 million subscribers to her main channel and almost half a million to her second – It's Lindsey Time. This second channel gives fans to behind-the-scenes access to her life.

Quick triv

When she entered *America's Got Talent* in 2010, Lindsey made the:

a) Quarter-finals   b) Semi-finals   c) Finals

Vlogger ID:	Joey Graceffa
Real name:	Joseph Graceffa
Born:	May 1991
Vlog Type	Drama and daily
Achievements:	Conceived, filmed, produced and starred in the award-winning web drama 'Storytellers'.

Even if you haven't ever clicked onto his channel, chances are you'll have seen Joey Graceffa on screen. He's extremely popular within the vlogging community – constantly popping up in collabs with other YouTubers. Joey has attempted the 'What's In My Mouth?' challenge with Zoella and talked about first impressions with Sprinkle Of Glitter, to name but a few. The star is a gamer, a singer, a short filmmaker and a colourful presenter who loves nail polish and lilac hair dye. He posts daily about everything from first dates to being a dog owner.

Quick triv

Joey's middle name is:
a) **Michael**   b) **Martin**   c) **Marcus**

Vlogger ID:	The Fine Bros
Real name:	Benny and Rafi Fine
Born:	March 1981 and June 1983
Vlog Type	Comedy
Achievements:	Featured on the websites of *Time*, *Variety* and *The Wall Street Journal*. Signed by Nickelodeon.

Ha! Ha!

The Fine brothers are new media pioneers. Not content with one little YouTube channel, they set up Fine Brothers Entertainment instead – a network focussed on bringing innovative and exciting content to the Internet. The boys are best known for their hilarious series 'React' where kids, adults and animals respond to a daft range of stuff. Their most popular clips include, 'Kids React To Adele' and 'Parents React To SnapChat'. They also film shot for shot remakes of real movies completely underwater, as well as running a regular series called 'Inappropriate Parents'.

Quick triv

The Fine Brothers also have a YouTube series called:
a) **Bloopers**   b) **Spoilers**   c) **Duffers**

Check your answers on page 96.

U.S. OF VLOG

Time to put some more fabulous American vloggers in the spotlight. These guys are YouTube big-timers – check them out!

LIFESTYLE

Vlogger ID:	Bethany Mota
Real name:	Bethany Mota
Creates:	Cute, colourful and varied clips – Bethany is the American Zoella. Her sunny personality shines through in her delivery.
She once:	Appeared as a guest judge on US fashion reality show *Project Runway*.

FASHION

Vlogger ID:	Clothes Encounters
Real name:	Jenn Im
Creates:	Gorgeous posts based on fashion and style. Jenn is the best at hauls and spotlighting the latest seasonal looks.
She once:	Had a part-time job serving ice cream at Baskin Robbins.

DIY AND BEAUTY

Vlogger ID:	My Life as Eva
Real name:	Eva Gutowski
Creates:	Beauty and lifestyle tips that teens can easily achieve. Eva posts lookbooks, hauls and easy to follow tutorials.
She once:	Starred on the front cover of the cool US magazine *Trend*.

PRANKS

Vlogger ID:	Roman Atwood
Real name:	Roman Atwood
Creates:	Hidden camera prank videos, such as the 'Grandma Gets Arrested' film where he had his mum arrested on her 70th birthday.
He once:	Filled his house with snow and Christmas trees to surprise his kids.

Vlogger ID:	Connor Franta
Real name:	Connor Franta
Creates:	Thoughtful emotional posts, but also lighter collab clips with his pals. We love his 'Never Have I Ever' with Miranda Sings.
He once:	Used to swim for the YMCA swimming club, becoming state champion in the mile event.

COMEDY

Vlogger ID:	Grace Helbig
Real name:	Grace Helbig
Creates:	Funny videos about modern life. Grace comments on Kanye West's style choices and teaches her mum about Netflix.
She once:	Took part in the 2005 Miss New Jersey USA beauty pageant. She made the semi-finals.

MUSIC

Vlogger ID:	The Piano Guys
Real name:	Jon Schmidt, Steven Sharp Nelson, Paul Anderson and Al van der Beek
Creates:	Amazing and moving videos where they put their own twist on modern classics such as Adele's *Hello*.
They once:	Claimed that they got into music because their parents insisted they learn instruments and made them practise.

GIRLS` ISSUES

Vlogger ID:	Ingrid Nilsen
Real name:	Ingrid Nilsen
Creates:	Advice for girls on how to survive sick days and break ups, plus 'Sense of Self' – a series about accepting your identity.
She once:	Showed viewers how to create gorgeous wavy hair using socks as curlers!

Around The World

Vlogging is a truly global phenomenon, but how world web wise are you? Find a pen, then match each vlogger to their home country.

Once you've finished, look up each star's content and write a couple of lines about what you learned about their unique vlogging style!

1

Jamie Curry – Jamie's World

COMEDY AND TEEN

2

Chika Yoshida – Bilingirl Chika

EDUCATION AND CULTURE

3

Erik Range – Gronkh

GAMING

4

Felix Kjellberg – Pewdiepie

GAMING

5 **Lauren Curtis**

BEAUTY

6 **Lilly Singh – Superwoman**

COMEDY

7 **Sanne Vliegenthart – BooksAndQuills**

BOOKS

8 **Marzia Bisognin – CutiePieMarzia**

LIFESTYLE

9 **Norman Thavaud – Norman Fait Des Vidéos**

COMEDY AND TEEN

A) SWEDEN   D) ITALY   G) THE NETHERLANDS

B) NEW ZEALAND   E) AUSTRALIA   H) GERMANY

C) FRANCE   F) CANADA   I) JAPAN

All of the answers are waiting on page 96!

LIVE IT, FILM IT!

Live, laugh, love... and film every second! Vloggers can't resist sharing the big moments in their lives, from graduating college, to first dates, weddings, births and even funerals. Ups and downs, highs and lows – it's all part of the life we all lead.

DON'T TELL ANYONE, BUT I'M ABOUT TO PROPOSE!

When Jim Chapman popped the question to long-term girlfriend Tanya Burr he did it in style. The romantic lad flew her over to New York for the weekend, then got down on one knee in Central Park. Although he stopped shy of filming the actual moment (some things have to remain private, right?), he vlogged about his intentions, filmed the run-up and posted sweet footage of the pair sharing milkshakes afterwards.

OUR FIFTH BABY!

The Shaytards love adding to their brood and filming the joy of each new arrival. Shay Carl filmed every breath of the run-up to the birth of his fifth child. The action started at 4am when he and Colette drove to the hospital, then ran right through to to the moment when the nurse handed newborn Daxton to his proud and exhausted mum.

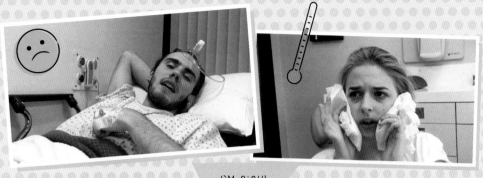

I'M SICK!

Unfortunately everybody gets ill every now and then, but vloggers like us to know that it's OK to feel less than your best. Many YouTubers have been brave enough to show the real people behind the make-up, filming themselves when they are in bed or unwell. Some, including Alfie Deyes and Jenn McAllister, have even filmed themselves in hospital. Luckily we've also got to join the vloggers on the road to recovery, too.

WE'RE MR AND MRS

Beauty vlogger Patricia Bright posted all the deets from her big day in March 2012, cutting live footage with gorgeous photographic stills of her marriage to Mike. Excited fans got to see the bride's pre-wedding preparations, her walk up the aisle and the lively reception, too. Just gorgeous!

DARK DAYS

When the worst that can happen happens, it can be a desperate time for those left behind. Some people believe that sharing your feelings is much better than bottling it all up. YouTuber TomSka posted a series of videos documenting how he felt when fellow creator Edd Gould died of cancer. American family vloggers Bratayley also live-streamed the funeral of their son Caleb Logan so that viewers could grieve, too.

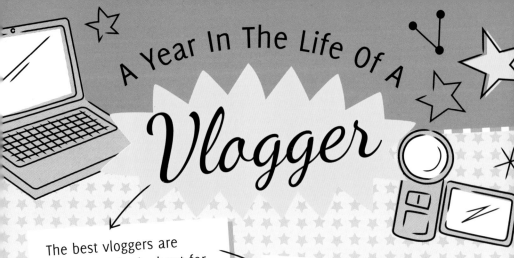

A Year In The Life Of A *Vlogger*

The best vloggers are always on the lookout for new material – fun things to do, try or make that will keep their subscribers coming back for more.

What brilliantly creative vlogging ideas can you think up for the year ahead? Use these diary dates to get you started.

New Year

New Year makes for some awesome vlogging content – buzzing parties, raucous singing and crazy dancing. Don't forget to film the fireworks as the clock strikes midnight!

Pancake Day

Toss them, eat them or get creative with your pancakes like Tyler and Hannah Hart.

Valentine's Day

Whether you have love in your life or not, it's time to talk romance. Or you could make yourself into a cute teddy, like Miranda!

Easter

Choccy, egg trees, cookies and cakes – Easter is always a yummy, scrummy date on the vlogging calendar.

Summer holiday

Whether you're sunning yourself in Southend, Southampton or South Beach, Miami, don't miss the chance to post all of your silliest, sandiest antics.

Halloween

Pumpkin carving, DIY costumes and out-there make-up – Halloween vlogging possibilities are endless!

Christmas

Happy Vlogmas! Now is the time to post your own on-screen advent calendar so that you and your viewers can countdown to the big day.

Happy birthday to me!

Birthdays are big news! Plan your extra-special vlog post here.

Just For Laughs

In a world full of serious news, it's great to know that we can always find something on YouTube, Vine or Instagram to bring a smile to our faces.

Feeling **silly**? Watch...

Smosh

Sometimes you need a quick fix of off-the-scale crazy. Head for Anthony Padilla and Ian Hecox's Smosh channel for some truly nutty sketches involving food battles, costumes and fake commercials.

Don't miss – 'Tom Cruise Is My Roommate' and 'Harry Potter Deleted Scenes'.

Bad day at school? Watch...

Miranda Sings

If you've had a mad day in the playground, you'll enjoy Colleen Evans' parody of a self-obsessed, highly-strung teen. Watch Miranda address her 'haters', give terrible make-up tutorials and screech out the latest tunes.

Don't miss – 'Siri Is A Hater' and 'I'm Quitting YouTube'.

Feeling **mischievous**? Watch...

Caspar Lee

Caspar is a consummate joker. He and roommate Joe Sugg are engaged in a hilarious prank war. Once Caspar even set up a secret camera, then phoned Joe pretending he'd had enough of living with him and wanted to move out.

Don't miss – 'Breaking Up With My Roommate' featuring ThatcherJoe.

Feeling down? Watch...

DanIsNotOnFire

Dan Howell's mix of 'epic fail' stories and funny advice clips make him the perfect pick-you-up. He's super-easy to relate to and you'll love his collabs with his best friend Phil. Dan says, "I let you laugh at my life so you can feel better about yours!" Job done.

Don't miss – 'List Of Reasons Why I'm An Awful Human Being' and 'How Not To Survive School'.

Parent stress? Watch...

Superwoman

Lilly Singh's sketches starring her as her over-protective Indian parents will take your mind off any rows you're having with your own folks! Lilly is great at making common issues funny. Her clip called 'How Girls Get Ready' has had 17.5 million views.

Don't miss – 'How To Stop Parents From Comparing Kids' and 'Instagram Pictures: My Parents React'.

Need a belly laugh? Watch...

NigaHiga

Ryan Higa has notched up more than 16 million subscribers and 2 billion views on his comedy channel. These stats all point to the fact that the guy is Funny with a capital F. Ryan's popularity stems from his wicked parodies of celebrity lives, funny how-to guides and 'Dear Ryan' Q&As.

Don't miss – 'How To Be Ninja' and 'Nice Guys'.

HOW MANY VLOGGERS DOES IT TAKE TO CHANGE A LIGHT BULB?
ONLY ONE, BUT IT'LL TAKE ALL DAY AS THEY FILM EACH STEP!

Put more laughter in your life with these funny guyz:

- Slomozovo
- Grace Helbig
- ShaneDawsonTV
- Fred
- Crabstickz
- Chewing Sand

Meet The
FITNESS VLOGGERS

Health and fitness is huge right now! We are logging on in our millions to pick up tips from expert vloggers. Here are just some of the best...

Carly Rowena

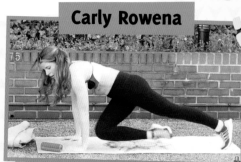

The Lean Machines

You may think one of these super-buff boys looks familiar. That's because one half of Lean Machine is John Chapman – brother of Samantha, Nicola and Jim. When his big sisters began Pixiwoo and twin Jim got into YouTube, personal trainer John thought he'd bring his passion for fitness to the table. He hooked up with friend and fellow trainer Leon Bustin and the pair began posting content that aimed to show that being healthy can be fun.

Subscribe if... you want to kickstart healthy habits and learn how to workout at home.

Carly has a growing following on YouTube and was recently snapped up by the people who manage the careers of Zoella and Tanya Burr. Her clips are really well produced and signposted so it's simple to find the specific hints and tips that you're looking for.

Subscribe if... you want fab abs. Carly is great at exercises that hone specific body parts and she has some top tips on how to get a six-pack.

My healthy vlog

Interested in health and fitness? How would your vlog look and feel? Use the space on the right to start planning!

Deanne Love

Ever fancied learning how to hula-hoop? Check out Australian, Deanne Love's, YouTube channel! Deanne posts regular tutorials to get viewers hooping for fitness, as well as teaching the art of freestyle hoop dance.

Subscribe if... you're a total beginner, novice or even an advanced hooper. Leanne has tips and tricks to suit all levels.

The Body Coach TV

SaskiasDansSchool

Joe Wickes, aka The Body Coach, has become the fitness trainer to watch. The videos on his YouTube channel, TheBodyCoachTV, focus on high intensity training. On Instagram Joe posts high energy mini-vids showing him cooking up a storm or demonstrating workout moves.

Subscribe if... you love super-quick healthy meal tips.

There are loads of great dancers who are also YouTubers, such as Maddie Ziegler from Dance Moms. If you want to get in on the act and can't get to a class, Saskia's Dance School is the place to go. There are fantastic, step-by-step tutorials showing you how to nail amazing hip-hop and street routines.

Subscribe if... you and your friends want to learn a group dance to kill it at the school disco.

Keep It In The Family

Did you know vlogging can bring you closer to your family? It's a great activity to do with the people who you love. These family vloggers all post content with their nearest and dearest.

The Shaytards

Shay Carl Butler began posting vlogs to his channel, Shaytards, back in 2007. At the time he was an overweight dad, living in rural Idaho, USA. Fast forward eight years and he is now slicker, slimmer and a multi-millionaire. Shay has filmed his entire weight loss journey as well as every cough, sniff and breath of his life with wife Collette and their five children Gavin, Avia, Emmi, Brock and Daxton.

Most watched vids: 'A Baby Is Born' and 'We Have Lice'.

The Saccone-Jolys

Irish couple Jonathan and Anna are heading towards 1.5 million subscribers on their YouTube channel thanks to their daily vlogging and mega-cute kids. The couple post about family life – showing everything from their kids' ballet classes to supermarket visits and accidentally crashing the car.

Most watched vids: 'Lives Changed Forever', 'Our Wedding' and 'Zoella's Our New Nanny'.

The Michalaks

Young newlyweds, Hannah and Stefan Michalak, are gaining in popularity every day thanks to their fun family video diaries featuring their cute son Grayson and Stef's dad. The couple are great on camera having both worked in the media, and post very professionally produced clips.

Most watched vids: 'Baby Spa Date' and 'I Think I'm Pregnant'.

Judy Travis is a beauty enthusiast, a wife to Benji and a mum to three adorable girls – Julianna, Miya and Keira. Her posts focus on the funny things that her kids say and do, her beauty picks, and even arguments with her husband.

Most watched vids: 'Cutest Baby Talk Ever', 'Delivering Identical Twins' and 'Baby Kicks Dad In The Face'!

ItsJudysLife

Which family members would you most like to vlog with?

What is cool about your family?

It's A Girl Thang

Girl power has truly hit the Internet – there are loads of fab sister acts online. Sometimes the girls choose to vlog under one username, others have their own separate channels, but pop up in each other's clips. However they choose to play it, we love seeing how the sisters interact. Vlogging siblings chat, laugh, fall out and make up just like the rest of us!

How many of the sisterhood can you ID from these photos?

1

2

3

4

5

6

7

8

Check your answers on page 96.

Meet The VINERS

YouTube is not the only platform for people to post video content. If you like your posts short and snappy, how about a mini-vlog clip lasting... ooh, six to ten seconds? All of these stars have built online profiles just by posting looping videos on sites such as Vine, Instagram and Twitter.

Name:	Alicia Herber
Vine followers:	9 million
Known for:	Incredible animations including one of Beyoncé at the Superbowl made out of a splat of hot chilli sauce on paper.
What's next?	Internet superstardom!

Name:	Lauren Giraldo
Vine followers:	3.3 million
Known for:	Funny, spontaneous loops.
What's next?	A move to LA after graduating from high school.

Name:	Nash Grier
Vine followers:	12.5 million
Known for:	Cool skateboarding and basketball tricks.
What's next?	Ads – he's already starred in a McDonald's campaign.

Name:	Brittany Furlan
Vine followers:	9.8 million
Known for:	Recurring characters, like her airhead roommate, 'Barbie'.
What's next?	A sketch comedy show produced by Seth Green.

Name:	Amymarie Gaertner
Vine followers:	4.2 million
Known for:	Amazing dance clips featuring her cool choreography.
What's next?	More dance-based opportunities.

Name:	Ben Phillips
Vine followers:	1.3 million
Known for:	Pulling pranks on his hapless family and friends.
What's next?	Making his profile even bigger.

Name:	Alx James
Vine followers:	8 million
Known for:	Funny clips set inside his car.
What's next?	Reality TV beckons.

Name:	Cameron Dallas
Vine followers:	9.2 million
Known for:	Pranks like painting his apartment and everyone else inside it.
What's next?	A flourishing film career.

Name:	Logan Paul
Vine followers:	9 million
Known for:	Over-the-top, hilarious mini-clips.
What's next?	More Shorty award nominations and wins!

Name:	Andrew Bachelor (aka King Bach)
Vine followers:	15 million
Known for:	Collabing on some of some of the most popular vines ever.
What's next?	A career in TV. He already films shows for MTV and Showtime.

An **A-Z** Of Vlogging

A is for Amity Fest

The biggest UK vloggers on our doorstep? We're there. Tickets to this annual festival featuring Zalfie and co are hot, hot, hot!

D is for 'Draw My Life'

This Internet video craze sees vloggers drawing figures on a whiteboard and filming it in fast-motion.

B is for Book signings

Big name vloggers are being snapped up for publishing deals all the time. Book signing events are a great place to meet your favourite star in person (and bag an epic selfie).

E is for Editing

A vital skill for any would-be vlogger, good editing enables you to cut out embarrassing slips, trips or spills so that your content becomes slick and watchable.

C is for Challenges

From blindfolded make-up contests to the Bean Boozled challenge, crazy tests pop up all the time online. YouTube would be a duller place without them!

F is for Fan family

That's us! Any creator worth their vlog knows the value of the fans. Many think of them as a family that they like to talk to every day.

G is for Granny vlogger

Vloggers come in all shapes, sizes and ages – sisters, brothers, daughters and sons, mothers, fathers and grandparents. Beauty Vlogger Melissa55 has almost 25,000 subscribers. She's also 60 years old and has 7 grandkids!

J is for Job

Vlogging may start off as a hobby, but it's worth remembering that some vloggers do manage to turn filming clips into a full-time job, using the money they make from the adverts that YouTube places on their channel.

H is for Hauls

Haul videos, where vloggers talk viewers through their purchases, are one of the most popular vlogging trends. They can be used in any type of clip – from beauty and fashion to DIY.

K is for KSI

Big shout out to this multi-talented UK vlogger – he can turn his hand to rapping, comedy and gaming. KSI is the only UK star to be included in the top 10 richest vloggers in the world.

I is for Imagination

You'll need buckets of this if you're going to be a vlogger, so that your content stays fresh and interesting. You'll also need to take inspiration from other vlogs, news stories and the world around you.

L is for Lighting

Great lighting can make or break a vlog. Most content creators advise using as much natural light as possible and sitting near a window.

M is for Music

A gorgeous background track can levitate an otherwise unremarkable vlog entry to something special. Just be careful not to use music without proper permission!

P is for Pranks

...and pranksters. Joe Sugg, Caspar Lee, Smosh, BFvsGF spend a lot of time and effort thinking up clever and hilarious practical jokes for our amusement.

N is for Niche

You need to find yours before setting up a channel. Some people, like Alfie Deyes, have a broad theme, whilst others, like TheSlowMoGuys, have chosen a very specific angle.

Q is for Quality

And quantity, too! A good vlogger never sacrifices the quality of their content for the number of clips that they post. However, they also understand that they need to post regularly in order to keep subscribers happy.

R is for Roommates

Roommates Joe Sugg and Caspar Lee often post together, while most vloggers upload regular clips featuring their best pals. Vlogging is even more fun when you do it with friends!

O is for On the road

We love to follow the antics of our fave vlogging stars as they travel the globe – whether they're dedicated nomads like Louis Cole, honeymooners like Tanya Burr and Jim Chapman, road trippers like Caspar Lee, or are on tour like Tyler Oakley and MirandaSings.

S is for Subscribers

This is the number of people who love your content enough to sign up to your channel.

W is for Wi-Fi

This clever technology can make or break our day. The Wi-Fi's down? Disaster! There's no Wi-Fi? I can't even!

T is for Twins

Who doesn't love a twin vlog? Step forward Jack and Finn Harries, Niki and Sammy Albon, Austin and Aaron Rhodes and Lucy and Lydia Connell. Double the vloggers, double the content, double the fun.

X is for XOXO

The shorthand for kisses and hugs has made its way into many a vlogger's username. Jennxpenn also added the 'X' to her name because there was already another Jenn Penn on YouTube.

U is for Username

Every vlogger needs one. Whether you plump for the obvious (Jim Chapman), the cutesy (MayBaby) or the weird (Pewdiepie and Chewing Sand), your name is important, so choose well!

Y is for YouTube

There are other outlets for vloggers, but YouTube is the original and the best. There's no other site quite like it for giving a platform to self-expression and creativity.

V is for VidCon

The world's largest gathering of people who love the new culture of online video. VidCon is held in California every summer. It features top creators, workshops and plenty of meet and greets.

Z is for Zoella

Few can compare to the queen of vlogging. With 10 million YouTube subscribers and rising, Zoe Sugg, we salute you!

Quick Pic Quizzes

How well do you know your YouTube stars?

Put your vlogging knowledge to the test!

Just the two of us

Match these YouTubers with their on-screen partner or partners.

1
DAN HOWELL

2
IAN HECOX

3
OLI WHITE

4
SAMANTHA CHAPMAN

a
CASPAR LEE

b
NICOLA CHAPMAN

c
PHIL LESTER

d
ANTHONY PADILLA

e
JOE SUGG

WhoTube?

Whose faces have been scrambled here?

a

b

c

d

Banner biz

There's some cool channel art around.
Can you match each YouTuber to their banner?

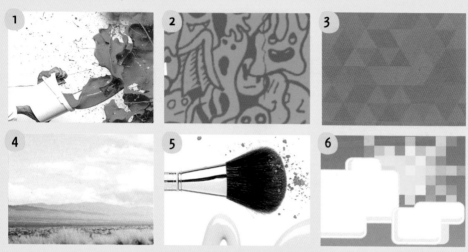

Finding it tricky? Don't go online quite yet!
All the names you need are in this box.

TOM FLETCHER   STAMPY LONGHEAD   LISA ELDRIDGE

THESLOWMOGUYS   FUNFORLOUIS   POINTLESSBLOG

Collab, much?

Use a pen to make a web between the YouTubers who have filmed collabs.

Now flip to page 96 to reveal the answers!

TRENDING NOW...

Where would our fave vloggers be without new tags and trends to add some pizzazz to their channels? The bigger a vlogger becomes, the more pressure there is to upload fresh, laugh-laden content. Luckily, there is always a new challenge surfacing online. How many of these have you watched or tried?

Blindfolded YouTuber drawing challenge

Blindfolded challenges are really popular and are usually totes hilarious. The latest craze is to take a list of scenarios and a list of famous YouTubers, put on a blindfold then draw a line to combine the two. Like the idea of Zoella riding a unicorn, or Tyler Oakley having a baby, anyone?

WATCHED IT ☐   TRIED IT ☐

Bean Boozled

Bean Boozled is like Russian Roulette with sweets. The idea is simple. You buy a packet of flavoured beans, then take it in turns to eat them. It sounds easy – except that vloggers are just as likely to get a rotten egg sweet as a strawberry sundae one. Bleurgh!

WATCHED IT ☐   TRIED IT ☐

Never have I ever...

The oldies are often the goldies! This game has been played for decades, but it always throws up surprises, shocks and laughs. Each player has to admit or deny a series of statements that could vary from, 'never have I ever peed in the shower' to, 'never have I ever been late for school.'

Careful!
Some YouTube trends can be messy, dangerous or both. Ask an adult before attempting to copy any stunts that you have seen online.

WATCHED IT ☐   TRIED IT ☐

No thumbs

Hugely popular among the US community, this challenge shows just how indispensable your thumbs are! Players ask a third person to use sticky tape to bind their thumbs to the palms of their hands, leaving them with only four usable fingers. The players then battle to be the first to complete a series of simple tasks such as opening a bottle of water.

WATCHED IT ☐ **TRIED IT** ☐

Eat it or wear It

This one can get very, very gooey... and messy. Players pull the name of a sticky yet potentially yummy ingredient out of a hat. It could be honey, chocolate sauce, golden syrup, jam, peanut butter, lemonade, or even squirty cream. Afterwards, they have to choose another slip of paper that will decide whether they have to eat it or wear it. The rest is obvious!

WATCHED IT ☐ **TRIED IT** ☐

The real me (stripped down) challenge

YouTubers love to talk, so it's not surprising that this challenge has been increasing in popularity recently. The idea is to have the camera rolling for ten minutes while you chat off the cuff, without any scripting or rehearsing. Afterwards, the clip must be posted without any cuts, edits, on-screen titles or music.

WATCHED IT ☐ **TRIED IT** ☐

Me, me, meme

A meme is a concept or idea that spreads virally from one person to another via the Internet. It can be a video, but the most common memes are pictures with funny captions. The rise of social media sites like Twitter, Instagram and Vine have seen an explosion in memes. In the past year a song by Awolnation called *Run* sparked a new Vine meme where people would cue the music and then run away from something or someone. Over on Twitter, Ellen DeGeneres' selfie of her surrounded by film stars on Oscar night sparked countless spoof memes.

Go With The Flow

Still trying to find your perfect vlogging style? Use this flowchart to help you! Put your finger on the START, then follow the YES/NO answers all the way to the end.

YES

MY STYLE IS FLAWLESS

I HAVE VLOGGING SIBLINGS

NO

NO

NO

YES

YES

I LIKE TO COOK

I LOVE TO BE MYSELF

NO

NO

YES

YES

FLAMBOYANT CHAT

Tyler is your vlogging icon. Like him you're naturally flamboyant and have your own personal style going on.

PRACTICAL BEAUTY

You look up to Tanya – you may be stylish, but you're also a practical vlogger who can cook up a storm in the kitchen.

HONEST STYLE

Zoella is your vlogging queen! You share her interest in style and make-up, as well as her shyness and honesty.

START

I CAN BE SHY

NO → I'M A NATURAL HOST

YES → I'M A HOME BIRD

I'M A NATURAL HOST → YES → I'M INTO MAKE-UP TUTORIALS

I'M A HOME BIRD → NO → I'M HAPPY LIVING OUT OF A SUITCASE

I'M INTO MAKE-UP TUTORIALS → YES

I'M INTO MAKE-UP TUTORIALS → NO

NO

YES

I'D LIKE TO VLOG DAILY

YES

NO

SHOWBIZ HILARITY

Miranda's definitely your bae. You're a clown who loves to act, sing and laugh – at yourself and others.

FRIENDLY FUN

You're so Joe! Although shy at heart, you are easily brought out of yourself. You're fun, popular and way too busy to film every day!

NEW ADVENTURES

Louis is your man – you share his passion for travel and can't wait to explore the world and meet its people.

Meet 'N' Greet

Want to get up close and personal with the vloggers who inspire you? There are several events worldwide that allow you to do just that. Start saving now or add a ticket to the top of your next birthday or Christmas list!

Digi Tour

Held: Throughout the summer
Venue: Various, around the USA and Canada
Expect: Creative collabs with the biggest stars from Vine, Twitter and Instagram, as well as YouTube.
Find out more at: www.thedigitour.com

Summer In The City

Held: August
Venue: London Excel Centre
Expect: Big crowds. This is the UK's largest YouTube convention – there are live performances, talks, exhibits and a lot of merch!
Find out more at: www.sitc-event.co.uk

VidCon

Held: June
Venue: Anaheim Convention Centre, California
Expect: The trip of a lifetime – it's LA, baby!
Find out more at: www.vidcon.com

#In The Loop

Held: TBC
Venue: The venue for the first ever UK VineCon is still being confirmed.
Expect: The opportunity to see your favourite Viners for more than six seconds.
Find out more at: www.itlevent.com

Amity Fest

Held: Dates to come
Venue: Brighton Dome and other venues around the UK.
Expect: To see Zalfie and the rest of the best UK vloggers.
Find out more at: Twitter @Amityfest

VidfestUK

Held: May
Venue: Excel Centre, London
Expect: The cream of creative, particularly those working in animation and with web series like TomSka and the Yogscast.
Find out more at:
Twitter @VidFestUK

VLOGGING DAY TRIPS

If you can't get to meet your vlogging idols at an event, then try walking a mile in their shoes. Here are some of their favourite places! We can't guarantee you'll run into them, but you never know…

Brighton

Head for the seafront and take a stroll on the promenade, Zalfie are often spotted walking their dog, Nala, there. Do some shopping in the Lanes area. It's rammed with cute and quirky boutiques.

London

Mingle with the fash pack and big vlogging names at London Fashion Week. Tanya Burr and Jim Chapman are regulars. Check out the film premières at Leicester Square. You'll need to arrive early, but the red carpet glitz is well worth the wait!

Northampton

When you've finished sampling the delights of the town, head to vintage store A Most Marvellous Place To Shop. You may spot Sprinkle Of Glitter and little Darcy having a mooch through the gorgeous trinkets.

Surrey

This beautiful county is also home to the Saccone-Joly family. Head up Box Hill or Leith Hill to take in the spectacular views. You might even get to wave at Jonathan, as he cycles through the leafy lanes!

Norwich

Stroll past the castle and the cathedral – you may just glimpse the Pixiwoo sisters on their way to the shops. Tanya Burr is often seen here too, shopping up a storm in Topshop and Lush. Visit Holkham beach, another fave haunt.

Over To You...

So you've finished this book – well done! Now you're an expert on this cool new way of communicating. You've been introduced to the Internet's breakout stars and been inspired by their creativity, too. You've taken quizzes, learned about trends and identified your favourite types of vlogger.

One day soon you may even be ready to start your own vlog. When you are, looking back through this book will help you pinpoint the kind of content, tone and style that you want to upload.

USE THIS SPACE TO WORK ON IDEAS FOR YOUR OWN CHANNEL ART AND USERNAME LOGO.

CHANNEL BANNER IDEAS

LOGO IDEAS

DON'T SPEND BIG BUCKS

"When I began, I started with just a webcam and my phone to make videos on. It would be really silly to shell out lots of money on really expensive cameras when you're not sure it's something you're going to stick at for the long run. So start small and work your way up." Louise Pentland (Sprinkle Of Glitter)

RESEARCH CONTENT

"Watch other YouTubers. Make the kind of videos that you enjoy watching. The more fun you have, the more fun people will have watching them." Alfie Deyes (PointlessBlog)

BRAINSTORM TO PREPARE

"It can be quite tricky to come up with a video idea that can be funny and entertaining, so at this point I usually turn to a pen and paper and write down anything that pops in my head or try and think of something interesting that's happened to me." Jim Chapman

SEARCH FOR STORIES

I try to cut out a small piece of my day and find a story. I make that story the underlining theme of that day's vlog." Casey Neistat

GET TO THE POINT

"If you waffle in your videos… you may find yourself sending your viewers to sleep. Which isn't a good thing." Joe Sugg (ThatcherJoe)

CHARISMA COUNTS

"A lot of people think being at the top means you have to be the best at a certain game. You don't. It's more about personality." KSI

LEARN TO SWITCH OFF

"Switch off when you need to. Give yourself time to chill out. Vlogging can make you feel you're always in front of the camera, but it's important to have some no camera days as well." Lily Pebbles

NEVER GIVE UP

Your first videos are probably going to be your worst so don't just give up. You'll get better as you go and your videos aren't going to be as great as someone who's been doing it for years. Don't get discouraged. It takes practice and time. Keep your head up and just keep trying." Joey Graceffa

ANSWERS

Pages 58–59
Best Of British
KSI b) Lamborghini
Niomi Smart a) Narcus
Jim Chapman c) Psychology
BubzBeauty c) 10 years

Pages 62–63
US Of Vlog
Michelle Phan c) Boston
Lindsey Stirling a) Quarter-finals
Joey Graceffa a) Michael
The Fine Brothers b) Spoilers

Pages 66–67
Around The World
1. b   2. i   3. h
4. a   5. e   6. f
7. g   8. d   9. c

Pages 76–77
Keep It In The Family
It's A Girl Thang
1. Veronica and Vanessa Merrell
   (MerrellTwins)
2. Jess and Stef Dadon (HowTwoLive)
3. Maddie (MaddieZiegler) and
   Mackenzie (MackZ) Ziegler
4. Elle (AllThatGlitters21) and Blair
   (JuicyStar07) Fowler
5. Lucy and Lydia Connell
   (LucyAndLydia)
6. Grace and Amelia Mandeville
   (MandevilleSisters)
7. Sam and Nicola Chapman
   (Pixiwoo)
8. Brooklyn and Bailey McKnight
   (BrooklynAndBailey)

Pages 86–87
Quick Pic Quiz
Just the two of us
1. c   2. d
3. a and e   4. b

WhoTube?
a) Marcus Butler   b) Zoella

c) PewDiePie   d) KSI

Banner biz
1. TheSlowMoGuys
2. Tom Fletcher
3. PointlessBlog
4. Fun For Louis
5. Lisa Eldridge
6. Stampy Longhead

Collab, much?
New vlogging collabs are happening
every day! You'll need to check out
YouTube to make sure you've got all
the latest pairings.